P9-BJK-935

Oriental Shorthair Cats

Stephanie Finne

Checkerboard
Library

An Imprint of Abdo Publishing
www.abdopublishing.com

www.abdopublishing.com

Published by Abdo Publishing, a division of ABDO, PO Box 398166, Minneapolis, MN 55439. Copyright © 2015 by Abdo Consulting Group, Inc. International copyrights reserved in all countries. No part of this book may be reproduced in any form without written permission from the publisher. Checkerboard Library™ is a trademark and logo of Abdo Publishing.

Printed in the United States of America, North Mankato, Minnesota.
032014
092014

THIS BOOK CONTAINS
RECYCLED MATERIALS

Cover Photo: Photo by Helmi Flick
Interior Photos: Glow Images pp. 5, 21; iStockphoto pp. 1, 11; SuperStock pp. 9, 17;
    Thinkstock pp. 7, 13, 15, 18–19

Series Coordinator: Bridget O'Brien
Editors: Rochelle Baltzer, Tamara L. Britton, Megan M. Gunderson
Art Direction: Renée LaViolette

Library of Congress Cataloging-in-Publication Data

Finne, Stephanie.
  Oriental shorthair cats / Stephanie Finne.
     pages cm. -- (Cats)
  Includes index.
  Audience: Age 8-12.
  ISBN 978-1-62403-325-4
1. Oriental shorthair cat--Juvenile literature. I. Title.
  SF449.O73F56 2014
  636.8'2--dc23
                    2013048625

Contents

Lions, Tigers, and Cats

All cats are members of the same family, **Felidae**. There are 37 species in this family. These include lions, tigers, and even house cats! Early cats were all wild cats. They were very efficient hunters.

Then about 3,500 years ago, ancient Egyptians began to tame these wild cats. The cats kept the Egyptians' food supply free of **rodents**. The Egyptians valued cats so much they worshipped them in temples.

Today, there are more than 40 different cat **breeds**. Like their ancestors, **domestic** cats are skilled hunters. But they also can be loving companions. One of these friendly breeds is the Oriental shorthair cat.

When you get home, your Oriental will greet you at the door. It will want to share its day with you!

Oriental Shorthair Cats

Oriental shorthair cats are related to Siamese cats. Siamese cats are known for their light-colored coats and dark-colored **points**. They were introduced to the United States in 1878.

In the late 1950s, Europeans **bred** solid-colored cats with Siamese cats. These new kittens were many different colors and patterns. At first, each new color and pattern became a new breed. Soon, there were too many colors to have separate breeds. So, all short-haired, non-pointed cats were called Oriental shorthairs.

In the early 1970s, US breeders began breeding these new cats. Four years later, the **Cat Fanciers'**

Oriental shorthairs are just like Siamese cats. The difference between the two breeds is that Orientals can be any color or pattern.

Association recognized this **breed**. By 1977, the breed had reached championship status. Two years later, there were 50 different recognized color and pattern combinations!

Qualities

Oriental shorthair cats are loving and **vocal**. They want to be near people. If given the attention they need, they will do anything to please their owners. They are unhappy if they are ignored.

Oriental shorthairs do not like to be alone. They like children, dogs, and other cats. They will soon become playmates with all family members. Most Orientals love everyone, jumping from person to person for attention.

These cats are very playful. They can also entertain themselves with simple toys, such as a cardboard box.

Oriental shorthairs are very curious and intelligent. They will open drawers, jump on shelves, or dig in bags to find hidden objects!

Orientals are perfect cats for people who want active, amusing pets!

Coat and Color

The Oriental shorthair's coat is glossy and lies close to the body. It is satin-like and short all over. This makes the cat easy to groom. A quick brush is all it needs.

This **breed**'s coat can be any color. Solid white, cream, red, ebony, blue, chestnut, lavender, cinnamon, or fawn are common. These nine colors can be combined to create many patterns. An Oriental's coat can be shaded, smoke, **parti-color**, **bicolor**, or **pointed**.

Some Oriental coats have the **tabby** pattern. There are four tabby patterns. Breeders cross cats with tabby coats with cats that have other patterns and colors. This can produce 112 different tabby combinations!

Currently, there are 281 different Oriental shorthair colors. No matter which one you choose, you will get a fun, colorful companion.

Because they can be so many colors, Oriental shorthairs are sometimes called rainbow cats!

Size

Like the Siamese cat, Oriental shorthair cats are long and muscular. They have thin bones. Members of this **breed** weigh 9 to 14 pounds (4 to 6 kg). Females are smaller than males.

The Oriental's head is a long, tapering wedge. It features almond-shaped eyes and large, pointed ears. Usually, the eyes are green. However, white or **bicolor** Orientals can have green or blue eyes. They can also be **odd-eyed**.

The Oriental's long, sleek body has long, slim legs. The oval-shaped front paws have five toes each. There are only four toes on each hind paw!

An Oriental's hind legs are longer than its front legs.

Care

Like all cats, your Oriental will require regular checkups with a veterinarian. The vet will examine your cat. And, he or she will give your cat any **vaccines** it needs. The vet can also **spay** or **neuter** your pet.

Just like its wild relatives, your Oriental will need to bury its waste. So, it will need a **litter box**. Don't forget to remove waste from the litter box every day.

Wild cats sharpen their claws on trees. Most houses don't have trees in them! A scratching post will give your Oriental something on which to scratch.

Remember, Oriental shorthair cats are very playful. And, active cats are less likely to gain weight. So, provide lots of toys for your feline friend.

Your Oriental shorthair will play fetch for hours!

Feeding

Part of caring for your cat includes providing a balanced diet. All cats are carnivores. They need to eat meat. A food that is labeled "complete and balanced" contains all the **nutrients** your cat needs.

There are different types of cat food. Canned foods are moist. Semimoist foods are softer than dry foods. Dry foods help clean your cat's teeth.

Your vet can help you determine which food is best for your cat. He or she can also help with a feeding schedule. Along with food and treats, be sure to provide fresh water for your cat. Cats need clean water every day.

Milk contains protein, but not all cats can drink it. It makes some cats sick.

Kittens

Most cats are able to mate at 7 to 12 months of age. After mating, female cats are **pregnant** for about 65 days. There are usually four kittens per **litter**. Having a litter is called kittening.

When kittens are born, they are helpless. They can't see or hear. They develop their senses after 10 to 12 days. At three weeks, they can walk around and explore.

The kittens learn and grow every day. For the first five weeks, kittens drink their mother's milk. Then, they are **weaned** onto solid food.

They are able to leave their mother at 12 to 16 weeks old.

An Oriental's colors may take some time to develop. **Tabby** colors can appear right away. Others may not appear until the kitten is one year old.

Cats of all ages sleep for many hours a day. It helps kittens grow.

Buying a Kitten

A kitten can demand a lot of attention. Orientals like to be near their human. They want to be a part of your daily life! Be sure you can give an Oriental shorthair cat a lot of attention.

Have you decided an Oriental is the right cat for your family? To find a kitten, search for a reputable **breeder**. Good breeders sell healthy cats. They can tell you the history of your kitten. They also provide **vaccines**.

When you find a breeder, look for a kitten that is active and curious. Check to be sure you are not allergic to the kitten.

When you bring home your cat, you will need some supplies right away. Your pet will need food and water dishes, food, and a **litter box**. Now you are ready to welcome your new Oriental shorthair into your family! Your pet will be a loving part of your family for 12 to 15 years.

Some cats like to go outside. However, indoor cats tend to be healthier and live longer.

Glossary

bicolor - having two colors.

breed - a group of animals sharing the same ancestors and appearance. A breeder is a person who raises animals. Raising animals is often called breeding them.

Cat Fanciers' Association - a group that sets the standards for judging all breeds of cats.

domestic - tame, especially relating to animals.

Felidae (FEHL-uh-dee) - the scientific Latin name for the cat family. Members of this family are called felids. They include lions, tigers, leopards, jaguars, cougars, wildcats, lynx, cheetahs, and domestic cats.

litter - all of the kittens born at one time to a mother cat.

litter box - a box filled with cat litter, which is similar to sand. Cats use litter boxes to bury their waste.

neuter (NOO-tuhr) - to remove a male animal's reproductive glands.

nutrient - a substance found in food and used in the body. It promotes growth, maintenance, and repair.

odd-eyed - having two different eye colors.

parti-color - having a dominant color broken up by patches of one or more other colors.

points - an animal's extremities, such as the feet, the ears, and the tail. A pointed coat features color on the points.

pregnant - having one or more babies growing within the body.

rodent - any of several related animals that have large front teeth for gnawing. Common rodents include mice, squirrels, and beavers.

spay - to remove a female animal's reproductive organs.

tabby - a coat pattern featuring stripes or splotches of a dark color on a lighter background. Individual hairs are banded with light and dark colors.

vaccine (vak-SEEN) - a shot given to prevent illness or disease.

vocal - likely to express oneself with the voice.

wean - to accustom an animal to eating food other than its mother's milk.

Websites

To learn more about Cats,
visit **booklinks.abdopublishing.com**. These links are routinely monitored and updated to provide the most current information available.

Index